Lavender Lines: broken petals and fresh buds

Rachel Kiskaddon

BookLeaf Publishing

India | USA | UK

Presentation by *BookLeaf Publishing*

Web: www.bookleafpub.com

E-mail: info@bookleafpub.com

ISBN: 9789360941079

First edition 2024

ACKNOWLEDGEMENT

This book contains poems that were previously published by Moonstone Art Center (Poet Imposter, I, Woman, Esperanza, One Week, Dreaming from the Nest) and Poet's Choice (The Harder I Try). All poems were written by Rachel Kiskaddon. Thank you to the writing communities at Moonstone Art Center, Blue Stoop, and the Goggle Works who supported me to create, edit, and share these works at readings.

PREFACE

The poems in this book have been written and edited over a period of decades. Some of the thoughts and situations expressed are embellished by the author. The work depicts self-harm, depression, and suicidal ideation, that may not be appropriate for all readers.

Poet Imposter

Creative energy flows.

Brain waves to tongue,
to text on the page.

Rambling, muttering,
the phrases tumble out.

Do I even make sense?
Imposter syndrome in full effect.

Am I a poet, a writer, an artist
If no one knows it but me?

Without footprints, who will know I walked
here.

Birdcage

Locked in this cage
Of my own making
I stare out the window
Glimpses of sky and tree tops
That I will never touch
Unable to spread these wings

Moments replay of where it all went wrong
Mistakes I have made along the way

I should have never moved here
Not with you, not now
But I sealed my own fate
Put the nails in the coffin
I wait for it to be over.
Knowing I can't fly away.

Dreaming From the Nest

From her rooftop perch,
She gazed at the city.
Mesmerized by the bright lights.
Tracing the streets with her mind.
Believing she would know them all.
That she could conquer this town

A place Where Dreams Come True
Believing her dreams would too.
Naivety shone in her wide eyes,
Too blinded to see the broken dreams.
That litter the pot-holed streets
Of this unforgiving and cruel city.

All she needed was a push from the nest.

Inspired Stroll

Walking down the cobblestone street
Past boarded windows and bolted doors
Shattered glass lines the curb
shards glistening in the sun
In between the broken bricks
Catching my eye as I stroll

I take another slow drag
Pulling in the smoke and scenery
Taking photographs in my mind
To remember the moment
As a calm washes over me
I feel free to be myself
Listen only to inner ramblings
Releasing the pressures of society

I wander the unfamiliar street
Enjoying the warmth of the sun
Looking for inspiration,
Anything other than you.

White Cat in a Window

As I pass in my car
I glance and say hello
There she sits
A pretty white
Cat in a window

I remember that cat
When it jumped on the bed
I remember petting her
Listening for a hiss or purr.
I remember thinking
she would be ours.

Flash to Black

It happened in a flash
The squeal of tires
The crushing of metal
The smashing of glass
A body breaking in half
In an instant lives forever changed.

Where did I glance? Was it my phone?
How did this happen? What comes next?

I feel everything and nothing
Body is numb and still
My hair and ear all wet and sticky
Taste of metal, the blood in my mouth
Puddle forming as it flows
from me, a silent river

Who did I hurt? What is their name?
Where were they going? Are they ok?

Suddenly none of it matters.
Flashes of memories, family, friends, and lovers
Three decades of moments scroll by
Then blackness, the curtain call.

The Harder I Try

My life has escaped me
I don't know who I am
I don't know what I want

My relationship is crumbling
My bills are piling
My stress is mounting
My heart is breaking
My mind is unraveling

Nothing in life is going as it should
The harder I try the more I fail
With every upwind I fall
swiftly off course

Waiting for Someone

Waiting for someone
Someone to fill the holes
Holes in my heart
Heart of gold waiting to melt
Melt into love
"Love is all you need"
Need is the absence of want
Want to be loved
Loved by a boy or girl
Girls have the softest skin
Skin like a baby's bottom
Bottom of the bottle
Bottle which is never empty
Empty like my heart
Heart which has seen no love
"Love is all you need"
Need to quench this thirst
Thirsting for another drink
Drink to drown your thoughts
Thoughts that cloud your mind
Mind which is being abused
Abused as my broken heart
Heart that is filled with holes
Holes that are waiting
Waiting for someone to love
Love yourself.

Phase

You say it is just a phase.
I'm just looking for attention,
That I will grow out of it,
One day I will choose a side.
- I will choose a person.

You say that I will cheat,
That I want to many people,
I could have everyone, anyone.
How can I resist the temptation?
- I will be faithful to my partner.

You say I don't fit in here.
Not queer enough, not straight enough
Stuck in the middle between worlds,
A no man's or woman's land to wander alone.
        - I just want to love and be loved.

First Kiss

I am lost in a daydream
Recalling the night we kissed
And the wetness of your lips
Their fullness against mine
The taste of gum mixed with freshly applied
lipgloss

Then the excitement that filled me
With desire I could not understand.
Wanting only to explore you more
New cravings I never knew I had
A raging passion set ablaze by your kiss.

One Week

For one week I walked around with you.
In my belly, a tiny seed of life.

For one week I was aware of your presence,
And the preparations my body had made.

For one week I didn't drink,
Even though I knew it wouldn't matter.

For one week I thought about the possibility,
Of holding you in my arms.

For one week I was glowing
No longer an empty vessel, with you in my
womb.

When the week ended I didn't grieve you.
I knew I made the right decision for both of us.
I was your mother for one week, and that was
enough.

I woman

I, woman, have talent and tenacity.
Though you may see me as a pretty face
Though you may doubt my intelligence
Though you may say I am good, for a woman.

I am more than your assumptions
More than a wife, a mother, a daughter.
More complex than a Madonna or a Whore
I am a whole person who lives for myself.

Grief Shrouds

My grief is your sweater
I wear it some ten years later
To feel the warmth of your hug.
The power in your strong arms
I can't fill out the sweater
Or the space you left empty
But I stitched up the moth holes
And the holes left in me.

My grief is your jean jacket
Edges worn thin with love
It still smells like the garden
Five years later, and sweat in the collar
I rub my worries away on the frayed cuffs.
My heart lives on the thread bare sleeves.

My grief is a collection of shrouds I wear to
Remember you lived and I loved you.

Albatross

I can feel the weight of your body
Hanging around my shoulders

But I do not suffer the most
Our mother grieves the hardest
She alone knows the true loss

The woman who gave you life
Should never live to see it taken

Her tears falling to the earth
Where she buried her son
The heir to her Kingdom.

The same story replayed in all history
The crutch of all pain on Earth
Everyone knows the plight of a grieving mother.

Three Wishes

Some days I cannot stop the tears
This grief is overwhelming
Its too close to the holidays
Just weeks from the only anniversary
I wish to forget

No matter the number of years
It still stings, it still gives me pain
Life is too short and fleeting
You had so much left in you
I wish to give you mine

If only I could take your place
Our mother was right
when we fought and she said,
"I wish it were you instead."

Spitting Sticks and Stones

All the bad things you ever said
Are still ringing in my head
I recite them again and again
As I lay sobbing in my bed

You never knew how much I heard
How I took it all to heart
You never knew how much I hurt
Till it tore me apart

The words seem to have no meaning
As you shout them in my face
But all I grew up thinking was
How can I get out of this place?

Invisible Boulder

I haven't Failed, I haven't let you down
But I built a mountain in my head
Placing so many obstacles in my way

You cannot see them, they are invisible
Though they feel so real to me.
I climb and climb getting more tired each day

I finally lay down, and you don't know why
You didn't witness the uphill battle
So you just worry and wonder

Why can't you see the invisible boulders?

Rage in my Head

I am stuck
at a point
in life, where
I am angry. Wanting to
pick up a knife. To
hack away
at these emotions
and feelings,
with the cuts
I will begin
healing. In these
moments where
I am alone. These violent
thoughts fill me.

I am stuck
between life
and living. I
am stuck
unable to turn back.
The future filled
with dread. For
my one true friend is,
in my head. I am
stuck between

the time
of then and now. I am
stuck on
when and how. Can
I turn the page? Or
Just full of rage?
This is not the place,
I want to be. But
I am Stuck,
unable to get free.

Bloodletting

So fresh it bubbles as it comes out
A shock at first, but I did not shout.

When I see that line and feel the sting.
I am healed, I grow wings.

Little red rivers flowing over fists.
they drip into the sink from my wrists.

Strange how the pain feels so good.
It gives me a high no drug could.

Such a release when nothing else works.
When the drink or smoke won't numb what
hurts.

But this is no fix for minor afflictions
Bloodletting is reserved for major infections.

It may not be the cure, this truth I see
But my blood is poisoning me.

Esperanza

I have "hope" tattooed on my wrist
A simple word in black ink
To remind me all there is to live for
To pull me from darkness to the light

A dove flying with an olive branch
Towards land from rough seas
To rescue me from drowning,
To remind me there's a silver lining.

At 20 years old I gifted myself hope
After years of searching for the rainbow
The ink now a little faded and fuzzy
But the message still reads clear.

As the scars underneath heal,
I find a bit more hope each year.

Quiet No More

I must write
I must share
I must use my voice
      Quiet no more

I must sing
I must play
I must make music
      Quiet no more

I must paint
I must create
I must make art
      Quiet no more

I must shout
I must scream
I must call for help
      Quiet no more

The writer shares
The musician sings
The artist creates
The activist shouts
      we cannot stay quiet anymore.